# POWER OF PRAYER

## 31 DAY PRAYER DEVOTIONAL

*In His Presence the*
*Power of Meditation and Prayer*

**TRACY JACKSON**

Book Package and Publication
Leadership DevelopME, LLC: www.leadershipdevelopme.com



Books may be ordered through booksellers or by contacting:

Tracy Jackson
Website: www.powerofprayerexperience.com



ISBN: 9781716418549
Library of Congress Control Number: 2021912425

Printed in the United States of America

May the Lord reward you
for your kindness. Ruth 1:8

Thank you so much, for
your support.
God bless you abundantly
for being a blessing!

Stay connected with Tracy Jackson &
Power of Prayer Ministry at:

www.powerofprayerexperience.com

# *Table of Contents*

## *Praises for the Power of Prayer*

Tracy Jackson is "Power of Prayer" manifested; her prayer life has marked the foundation of her book and preparation for her ministry. This book will help you to realize that prayer is as important as sleeping, eating and breathing. I sincerely believe that after reading her book you will never be the same again. Your prayers will have more power and there will be a significant change in your life, if you follow the divine steps she has laid out in this commanding and powerful book. The Power of Prayer Devotional should be a part of your daily spiritual diet.

Evangelist LuVon Richardson

As a longtime friend, it has been my privilege to witness Tracy's passion and commitment to her God given gift of intercessory prayer. Through her life experiences she is able to articulate with keen insight the importance of connecting and communing with God on a daily basis. Prepare to be tremendously blessed and inspired by this amazing Power of Prayer Devotional book.

Diane Wade, Friend and Sister in Christ

# *Foreword from My Pastor*

The **Power of Prayer Devotional** is a very effective and useful tool to encourage and stimulate one's daily connection with God. One should never underestimate the spiritual impact of combining prayer and scripture. This devotional is essential, as it: evokes Christian commitment, excites biblical disciplines, and fosters personal dedication to establishing or maintain a godly relationship with Jesus Christ. In today's world where morals and values are waning the church at-large must seek to remain fastened to its core values which is the Word of God intertwined with the Power of Prayer.

Evangelist Tracy Jackson, THANK You, for answering the prophetic call to produce such relevant literature. The Trinity Temple C.O.G.I.C. family is blessed to have you as our Prayer Director and we celebrate this outstanding accomplishment to the body of Christ.

**Bishop Benjamin Stephens, III, M.Div, D. Min**
Trinity Temple COGIC, Senior Pastor
International Youth President, Church of God in Christ

# *Foreword from My Friend*

*Maya Angelou quoted: Every journey begins with a single step, and you have stepped out by faith to bless others with your gift, The Power of Prayer Devotional.*

Over the last 10 years I've had the opportunity to spend time with this prayer warrior, Tracy. Her love for prayer and God as she so affectionately calls her Heavenly Father "Daddy" has matured, developed and blossomed into a strong and secure believer. There is no doubt in my mind that she eats, drinks and sleeps a life of prayer. Prayer is not a second option, nor is it her Plan B. Tracy knows that going to God is her only option and her only Plan!

Her prayer life does not consist of me and my three or you and your four. Tracy's ministry of Prayer is of Global nature, it extends here in Kansas City, Missouri and reaches to foreign countries.

This 31-Day Power of Prayer Devotional is not bound by race, gender, or cultural. The young and the old alike can benefit from its content and expect a God encounter.

This life of prayer has allowed Tracy to remain focused and intentional with God. She can be parallel with the Sons of

Issachar, for they had wisdom and understanding regarding the purposes and plans of God.

The tone of our day will be set as we daily read the scriptures and mediate on the exposition of this book. We will find ourselves drawing closer to God and He drawing closer to us. Those of you that take the time to read this book will be rewarded with the jewels that lie within the pages. Enjoy!

***Supervisor Diane L. North***

Jurisdictional Supervisor
Missouri Western First International
Assistant Elect Lady of Evangelism
Church of God in Christ, Inc.

# *A Note from the Author*

*Continue earnestly in prayer, being*
*vigilant in it, with thanksgiving.*
*Colossians 4:2*

We cannot afford **not** to pray. We cannot survive without praying. Prayer is our lifeline.

*Do not be anxious about anything, but in everything, by prayer and petition, with thanksgiving, present your requests to God. Philippians 4:6*

The ultimate key to spiritual growth is spending time alone with God. This means taking the time to speak with God about whatever is on your heart and, even more importantly, allowing Him to speak to you.

One of the most deceiving lies of Satan is that we just don't have enough time to pray. However, all of us have enough time to talk on our cell phones, search the internet and tweet. We would be amazed at how much more time is available to us for prayer, if we spent less time on the internet, our cell phones and social media.

The most intimate communication is to pray to the only true and living Savior, Jesus Christ. We are wise if we choose to spend time alone with God in prayer—in a place without distractions or interruptions. This is a period suitable for us to relax completely and focus our attention fully on the Father and His Word.

We must be willing to wait in the Lord's presence until we receive God's directives or His words of consolation.

The power of prayer is not the result of the person praying. Rather, the power resides in the God who is being prayed to—our Heavenly Father. I John 5:14-15 declares, *"This is the confidence we have in approaching God: that if we ask anything according to His will, he hears us."*

If we know that He hears us - whatever we ask - we know that we have what we asked of Him. No matter the person praying, the passion behind the prayers, or the purpose of the prayer—God answers prayers that are in agreement with His will. God's answers are not always "yes", nor are they based on our timetable but He <u>always</u> answers in our best interest.

When our desires line up with God's will, when we pray passionately and purposefully according to His word, God responds **POWERFULLY!**

After many years of serving God with the mission of prayer, I present to you this devotional. There is so much for us to pray about and beseech the Lord about on behalf of our families, our friends and even ourselves. I pray that you find this daily dose of God's goodness refreshing to your soul and spirit.

**Author & Prayer Warrior**

# *How to Use This Devotional*

*The Power of Prayer Devotional* is a tool. No tool is of any value if it is not used. Therefore, we hope that this tool may be put to good use in your life. Moreover, the effectiveness of a tool depends on the familiarity the user has with it. Skill with any tool comes through experience. The more you use *The Power of Prayer Devotional* the more skillful you will become. *The Power of Prayer Devotional* is a form or a pattern. Almost everything we do that is successful follows certain patterns. It could be that the reason many Christians never develop a meaningful devotional life is that they have failed to discover a truly meaningful devotional pattern.

*The Power of Prayer Devotional* pattern consists of four elements:

1. Prayer
2. Bible Study
3. Meditation
4. Recording

The following information will help you to familiarize yourself with this plan.

**TIME ALLOTMENT** The amount of time you allocate to your devotions depends on you. It is best that you set aside a minimum amount of time each day (perhaps 20 to 30 minutes) at an established time. Discipline yourself to keep this schedule. On some days, the Spirit of the Lord may lead you into longer times in His presence.

**PRAYER TIME ACRONYM A-C-T-S** will become the prayer pattern for your devotional time.

1. **ADORATION** Your prayer time should begin with adoration of God for His excellent greatness.
2. Adoration is a time to praise and worship God for who He is. You will want to focus on one of the aspects of God's attributes, character, or nature. A list of these is provided in the back of this devotional guide. The worthiness of God to receive praise, glory, and honor is the focal point of adoration. At times, singing is appropriate during adoration.
3. **CONFESSION** must be a continual part of your devotional life. There must be the confession of known sins, sins of omission, and unforgiveness. Ask the Holy Spirit to perform His ministry of conviction by bringing any sins that you may have committed in the last twenty-four hours to your conscious mind. It is important to deal regularly with your personal sin and to keep short-term accounts with God. A continual cleansing is needed in some areas to wash

out the effects of sins committed by you or against you. You need to submit to God basic assumptions about yourself, your relationship, your mind, and your emotions. Pray for your personality structure daily by appropriating God's gift of grace and inner healing. Restitution may be required for some acts of sin. There may be someone's forgiveness you need to seek, or you may need to make right any wrongs you have committed.

4. **THANKSGIVING** is the offering of true gratitude to God for His blessings. Let a spirit of gratitude fill your heart. Begin your thanksgiving to God for the forgiveness and cleansing of your confessed sins, and then focus your attention on particular blessings from God. It is also good to periodically give thanks to God for your redemptive history. A redemptive history is what God's grace has been producing in your life (i.e., what God is doing in me, from where God has brought me, what God is teaching me).

5. **SUPPLICATION** is a time to express your petitions to God. This involves both intercession and personal requests. Intercession is your prayers to God on behalf of the *needs of others*. Personal requests are your petitions concerning *needs in your life*. It is important to present to God those things you will be facing in the next twenty- four hours.

**PRAYER LIST**: Provided in the back of this tool to assist you in praying specifically.

**MEDITATION:** Journal lines are provided to record any thoughts, concepts, or impressions for meditation each day.

**RECORDING:** Journal lines are provided each day to record any significant events from each day's devotional.

**JOURNAL LINES:** Additional journal lines are provided in the back of this tool for additional notes you may need have to fully capture any promptings from the Holy Spirit.

Now… I prayerfully submit to you 31 days of devotional topics as given to me by the Holy Spirit. I pray that you experience the ***Power of Prayer*** every day of your life.

# Day 1

## Power of Meditation and Prayer

*Continue in prayer, and watch*
*in the same with thanksgiving*
*Colossians 4:2*

Never underestimate the power of prayer. When you are praying according to God's will, your prayer is unstoppable. How do we know what is God's will? By careful study of Scripture. Jesus made to us this promise: "If you abide in Me, and My words abide in you, you will ask what you desire, and it shall be done for you" (John 15:7).

We immediately gravitate toward the latter part of that verse: *Ask what you desire, and it shall be done for you.* We love that, as though God were some sort of genie. But that isn't the case! We tend to forget about the first part of this verse: *If you abide in Me, and My words abide in you.*

...If we are walking in fellowship with God and studying the Word of God, then we will start praying according to the will of God. Then we will start seeing our prayers answered.

First John 5:14–15 says, "Now this is the confidence that we have in Him, that if we ask anything according to His will, He hears us. And if we know that He hears us, whatever we ask, we know that we have the petitions that we have asked of Him."

Therefore, we should never give up or back down. We need to keep praying. That is why Jesus said, "Ask, and it will be given to you; seek, and you will find; knock, and it will be opened to you" (Matthew 7:7). In the original language there is an ascending intensity to the terms. It is like starting with some politeness. Then you get more aggressive. And finally you are not letting go, like Jacob who wrestled with an Angel of God and refused to let go until He blessed him.

***Exercise the power of meditation & prayer.***

Don't give up.

**MEDITATION:** THOUGHTS, CONCEPTS, OR IMPRESSIONS FOR TODAY:

**RECORDING:** SIGNIFICANT EVENTS FROM TODAY'S DEVOTIONAL EXPERIENCE:

# Day 2

## In His Presence

*The one thing I ask of the Lord--the thing I seek most--is to live in the house of the Lord all the days of my life, delighting in the Lord's perfections and meditating in his Temple.*
*Psalm 27:4*

David loved to be in God's presence. He just couldn't get enough. That's a wonderful thing to realize.

In the Old Testament, under the covenant, the Jewish people were represented by the high priest who would go into the temple and offer a sacrifice to God.

The good news for us today is that we don't have to go to a building to have an encounter with God. Because of what Christ did on the cross at Calvary, we have access to the Lord anytime, anywhere. Hebrews 10:11- 12 says, "Under the old covenant, the priest stands and ministers before the altar day after day, offering the same sacrifices again and again, which can never take away sins. But our **High Priest** offered himself to God as a single sacrifice for sins, good for all time." We can enter into God's presence wherever we are.

Did you know that your personal car or truck can be a sanctuary? Why not use your time on the road to build yourself up spiritually? You could listen to Bible teaching or Christian music. By the time you arrive at your destination, you will have learned something and glorified God through your worship. You can encounter God *wherever* you are.

When you make the decision to fellowship with other believers, to worship the Lord, and to listen to the Word of God, this is a very good choice.

To be in God's presence was David's focus. No wonder he was called a man after God's own heart. The desire to be in God's presence was at the forefront of his life.

Today, you should desire to be ***in His presence***.

**MEDITATION:** THOUGHTS, CONCEPTS, OR IMPRESSIONS FOR TODAY:

**RECORDING:** SIGNIFICANT EVENTS FROM TODAY'S DEVOTIONAL EXPERIENCE:

# Day 3

## *When God Delivers You, There Is No Residue*

*"Look!" he answered, "I see four men loose, walking
in the midst of the fire; and they are not hurt, and the
form of the fourth is like the Son of God." 26 Then
Nebuchadnezzar went near the [f]mouth of the burning
fiery furnace and spoke, saying, "Shadrach, Meshach,
and Abed-Nego, servants of the Most High God, come
out, and come here." Then Shadrach, Meshach, and
Abed-Nego came from the midst of the fire. 27 And the
satraps, administrators, governors, and the king's
counselors gathered together, and they saw these
men on whose bodies the fire had no power; the hair of
their head was not singed nor were their garments
affected, and the smell of fire was not on them.*
*Daniel 3:25-27*

It would have been easy for the Hebrew teenagers Shadrach, Meshach, and Abednego to think that God may have forgotten about them. The king had given a decree that everyone should fall down and worship a golden image he had erected of himself. When certain music was played, everyone in the kingdom was ordered to lie prostrate in worship. But there, standing up defiantly like three sore thumbs, were the three Hebrew boys; Shadrach, Meshach, and Abednego. It was teenage rebellion channeled in the right direction.

The king, however, didn't like their rebelling. He was so enraged that he ordered his guards to heat the furnace seven times hotter. The heat was so intense that when the guards who took the three Hebrew teenagers to the brink of the furnace, they were overcome by the flames and died.

When the king took a hard look, and inside he saw four, not three, individuals walking around in the fire. Where was God in all of this? God, our Lord, was with Shadrach, Meshach, and Abednego in the fiery furnace.

We always say, "Lord, get me out of this. Keep me from problems, Lord." But the Lord is saying, "There are times when I will answer that prayer, and there are times when I will walk with you through the hard days. But know this: I will never leave you or forsake you."

Being a Christian doesn't mean you will never have another problem. Being a Christian doesn't mean that life will be easy. But it does mean a lot of amazing things. It means you will never be alone again - no matter what you face in life. Jesus promised to never leave you nor forsake you. Jesus Christ will be with you, interceding for you, helping you, and walking with you through life. Sometimes God delivers us from the trial, and sometimes He delivers us while in the trial.

**Watch God work! When God *delivers you, there is no residue.***

**MEDITATION:** THOUGHTS, CONCEPTS, OR IMPRESSIONS FOR TODAY:

**RECORDING:** SIGNIFICANT EVENTS FROM TODAY'S DEVOTIONAL EXPERIENCE:

# Day 4

## *Day & Night*

*Keep this Book of the Law always on your lips; meditate on it day and night, so that you may be careful to do everything written in it. Then you will be prosperous and successful."*
*Joshua 1:8*

What does it mean to "meditate" on God's Word?

When reading the Bible, God's Word, meditation is thinking the verse over and over; seeing it from different angles and praying about how to apply it to your life.

This is how we should meditate on God's Word. We start by thinking about what the verse says. We mentally chew on it, sinking in its meaning. Then, we look at the passage again and think of what else it could mean, and how it applies to our lives.

The Bible is often called the Living Word because it always applies to our lives and have many meanings. This is why we meditate on God's Word - to discover the many meanings and things we can learn from the Word to better ourselves.

Another way to meditate on God's Word comes from the Hebrew word for meditation: *hagah-* which means to quietly speak the words of the text over and over to yourself. This helps us to 1) memorize the verses so we can remember what we read and 2) bring revelation to the meanings we are looking for as we continue our daily lives. One time I was meditating on the verse 2 Corinthians 5:7, I suddenly realized that the verse said "if anyone is *in Christ*" instead of "anyone who prays for it, anyone who works towards it, etc." meaning that I didn't need to work towards being new, I was new from the second I returned to God, no matter if I felt differently or not.

So…read God's Word. Don't just read the words, <u>meditate</u> on it ***day & night*** and see how it applies to your daily life!!

God bless!

**MEDITATION:** THOUGHTS, CONCEPTS, OR IMPRESSIONS FOR TODAY:

**RECORDING:** SIGNIFICANT EVENTS FROM TODAY'S DEVOTIONAL EXPERIENCE:

# Day 5

## Don't Let Anger Win

*And "don't sin by letting anger control you." Don't let the sun go down while you are still angry, for anger gives a foothold to the devil.*
*Ephesians 4:26-27*

We've all done it! We've gotten angry. There are a lot of reasons to get angry. Anger can come to us from many different sources.

Anger in itself isn't necessarily bad. It's your response to anger that can make or break you in life. For example, you got angry that you didn't get a good grade on your math test and you used that anger to motivate you to study harder for the next test. That response to anger would be good. You channeled your anger into something productive, like studying harder for a test.

Sometimes, your response to anger can be bad. If you allow your anger to consume you- you may do things you regret. The story of Cain in Genesis four is a good example of this. Cain got angry with his brother Abel and that anger drove him to ultimately kill Abel.

The Lord asked Cain, "Why are you angry? Why does your face look sad? You know that if you do what is right,

I will accept you. But if you don't, sin is ready to attack you. That sin will want to control you, but you must control it."

Cain said to his brother Abel, "Let's go out to the field." So they went to the field. Then Cain attacked his brother Abel and killed him. - Genesis 4:6-8 (ERV)

Cain made a bad decision out of anger. He chose to kill his brother Abel. Now, we know that killing someone is wrong, and most of us aren't tempted to kill someone, but what choices do you make when someone gets something you feel is unfair? Do you talk about them behind their back? Give them the silent treatment? Or maybe try to get even with them?

Doing these types of things will not help you in the long run. It might make you feel better in the moment, but trying to get even or not treating someone nice isn't the right way to respond to anger. When you get angry, you have a choice to make. Will you sin when you get angry and do something you may later regret, or will you channel that anger into something positive in your life?

"When you are angry, don't let that anger make you sin," and don't stay angry all day. - Ephesians 4:26 Pray that when you get angry, you *choose* not to get even or hurt someone else. *Choose* instead to channel your anger into something positive. Make the right choice - ***don't let anger win.***

**MEDITATION:** THOUGHTS, CONCEPTS, OR IMPRESSIONS FOR TODAY:

**RECORDING:** SIGNIFICANT EVENTS FROM TODAY'S DEVOTIONAL EXPERIENCE:

# Day 6

## *Keep Your Stride*

*But those who wait on the Lord*
*Shall renew their strength;*
*They shall mount up with wings like eagles,*
*They shall run and not be weary,*
*They shall walk and not faint.*
*Isaiah 40:31*

Hitting your stride is that place where you feel comfortable. The beginning of any workout plan is always the hardest. The muscles in your body are resisting the effort. For runners, the lactic acid in your legs builds up and needs to be worked out. That pain is a signal your muscle is using to let your brain know it's running out of energy. This pain signal typically comes well before your body is tired. Once you push through it, you will begin to hit your stride and you will experience the best part of running, the Runners Euphoria. It is that elated feeling that energizes every part of your life. We can experience a similar feeling as we hit our stride in walking with Christ. As we push through the early resistance, we feel closer to Him that in turn, affects other areas of our life. We want to get to the point where we are hitting our stride.

Establishing your rhythm and hitting your stride takes time. The runner's euphoria doesn't come until you have some mileage behind you. The same is true for our walk with Christ. At first, it is difficult to establish a rhythm, we don't feel like we are making progress, but after a couple of weeks, it becomes part of the norm. If we miss a day, it feels like there is a void in our day. As we travel the path to a fresh start, we will become more aware of the unceasing love of God.

This is greater than any runner's victory. The fruit of God's love in our life is joy.

Hitting your stride takes perseverance. Be steadfast in your journey with Christ. Some mornings you will wake up and not feel it. If you push through the fog, you will discover what God has for you. You will find his steadfast love and faithfulness for you. A daily walk that is filled with the joy of the Lord is greater than anything you can experience here on earth. So, ***keep your stride.***

**MEDITATION:** THOUGHTS, CONCEPTS, OR IMPRESSIONS FOR TODAY:

**RECORDING:** SIGNIFICANT EVENTS FROM TODAY'S DEVOTIONAL EXPERIENCE:

# Day 7

## Persecuted But Not Forsaken

*But we have this treasure in earthen vessels that the excellence of the power may be of God and not of us. We are hard pressed on every side, yet not crushed; we are perplexed, but not in despair; persecuted, but not forsaken; struck down, but not destroyed.*
*2 Corinthians 4:7-9*

New covenant servants (followers of Jesus Christ) are "earthen vessels" (ordinary clay pots). Yet, in the container of their redeemed humanity dwells "this treasure" (the Son of God Himself). This arrangement calls for the treasure (Jesus), not the vessels (you and me), to be the object of all trust and the recipient of all glory: "that the excellence of the power may be of God and not of us." Appropriately, the Lord has also arranged a process that magnifies the treasure.

This process involves the everyday pressures of life, which comes from all sides. "We are hard pressed on every side, yet not crushed." Clay pots cannot withstand much pressure, but the treasure within us (Christ) is able to keep us from being smashed. "Be strong in the grace that is in Christ Jesus" (2 Timothy 2:1)

The process that draws attention to the treasure also involves many perplexities. "We are perplexed, but not in despair." We face difficult decisions and impossible issues, but our Wonderful Counselor protects us from hopelessness: "in whom are hidden all the treasures of wisdom and knowledge" (Colossians 2:3).

Persecutions are included in the process: "persecuted, but not forsaken." People accuse us, misunderstand us, or lie about us; still, we know we are not abandoned by our Lord who lives within us. "For He Himself has said, -'I will never leave you nor forsake you'" (Hebrews 13:5).

Even catastrophes are a part of the process that magnifies the treasure who dwells in us: "struck down, but not destroyed." Circumstantial upheavals and overwhelming heartaches occur, but the Lord stabilizes our souls. "They confronted me in the day of my calamity, but the LORD was my support" (Psalm 18:18). Thus, life comes at us like an overpowering military tank, ready to flatten us. There is no natural hope, because clay pots can't handle tanks. Yet, as the dust clears, the flower pot of our lives can remain intact (if we are trusting in the able and faithful One who lives in our hearts). There is no attacking tank that can overcome the Lord Jesus Christ. "He who is in you is greater than he who is in the world" (1 John 4:4).

***You will survive persecution knowing that you are not forsaken.***

**MEDITATION:** THOUGHTS, CONCEPTS, OR IMPRESSIONS FOR TODAY:

**RECORDING:** SIGNIFICANT EVENTS FROM TODAY'S DEVOTIONAL EXPERIENCE:

# Day 8

## *I've Got to Win*

*He canceled the record of the charges against us and took it away by nailing it to the cross. In this way, he disarmed the spiritual rulers and authorities. He shamed them publicly by his victory over them on the cross.*
*Colossians 2:14*

"Finished" is the word we use after a job is done. It is a word that says we don't need to work anymore, because it is done. "Finished" is also the word Jesus used from the cross. He said, "It is finished!" (John 19:30). In other words, "It is accomplished!"

The devil was victoriously defeated at the cross of Calvary—and that is something he doesn't want us to know. Referring to His impending crucifixion, Jesus said, "The time for judging this world has come, when Satan, the ruler of this world, will be cast out." Through His death, Jesus destroyed the one who had the power of death. When we put our faith in Jesus Christ, the stronghold of Satan is broken. He cannot control us. We can rest in the finished work of Christ.

When we face spiritual battles, we are not fighting *for* victory; we are fighting *from* it. We don't fight to get victory. We fight because it has already been obtained. We don't need to pray, "Lord, give me victory." Rather, we should pray, "Lord, I have victory, and I will live accordingly." As Romans 8:37 tells us, "Despite all these things, overwhelming victory is ours through Christ."

We can win in the spiritual battle. We can overcome the enemy. I am not saying we will win every skirmish and every conflict, but I am saying we will win the war. I am not saying we will never sin and will never stumble, because we will. We all will. But we can win the battle overall, because we stand in the righteousness of Christ.

So when the devil tries to strike that fatal blow against you, it no doubt will be repelled, because you are standing right with God ***and you've got to win.***

**MEDITATION:** THOUGHTS, CONCEPTS, OR IMPRESSIONS FOR TODAY:

**RECORDING:** SIGNIFICANT EVENTS FROM TODAY'S DEVOTIONAL EXPERIENCE:

# Day 9

## *Time Is Too valuable*

*Teach us to realize the brevity of life,*
*so that we may grow in wisdom.*
*Psalm 90:12*

Have you ever felt that time was slipping through your fingers like grains of sand through an hourglass? I am sure that we all know that feeling. Historians use the expression, "the sands of time," when they write about a certain passage of events.

Let's talk about time. What is it? It's been said "it [time] is a measure of existence or the passing of events that irreversibly proceeds from the past, to the present, and on into the future." Time can be divided into days, hours, minutes and seconds. Days become months and years, but actually "time" is only the moment we have right now. Although time can be measured, it can't be stored. When a moment is gone, it is gone forever. You can plan the future and hold memories of the past, but "now" is all the time you and I possess. Therefore, we shouldn't waste that time by procrastinating. When we do, time passes and we will have accomplished nothing with our lives.

*God has given us 24 hours in each day.* Solomon said in Ecclesiastes 3:1-2 that there is a time for everything in the life of any individual. If we are to be successful, as God intends, then every moment must count. The Bible says it is the sluggard who wastes time. Wise people make wise use of time. The book of Revelation tells us that when we all step into eternity, time will be no more. But until that last day, it is God's desire for His people to build wisely upon the framework He has given to us.

How we choose to spend our time will determine our success or failure; our work and our reward, not only now but also in God's eternal kingdom. God wants us to achieve something. When we are good stewards of our time, we can achieve all God has for us to do.

Joshua was a man of God, chosen to lead the children of Israel into the Promised Land. Taking possession of the land required that he fight a battle against the Amorite kings. Joshua and his men were doing their part and continued the battle throughout the day. Daylight was waning and Joshua was running out of time to finish the battle. He cried to the Lord for help asking Him to lengthen the day for him so he could fight to the finish. And God did exactly that (Joshua 10:12,13). What a way to get the most out of your day. You see, when you have done your best, you can even ask God for miraculous help.

*Make choices to treat time as precious*. Now, that's the choice driven life because ***time is too valuable!***

**MEDITATION:** THOUGHTS, CONCEPTS, OR IMPRESSIONS FOR TODAY:

**RECORDING:** SIGNIFICANT EVENTS FROM TODAY'S DEVOTIONAL EXPERIENCE:

## Day 10

---

# *The Will to Press*

*I press toward the mark for the prize of*
*the high calling of God in Christ Jesus.*
*Philippians 3:14*

A life without a goal is like the captain of a ship without a map and a compass. His ship will just drift aimlessly from day to day hoping to arrive somewhere. The apostle Paul set for himself a goal! He pressed forward in search for his goal -- he pressed toward the mark of the high calling in Messiah! He had a clear direction of where he was going and he was focused on the Lord! How much more should we!

By setting a goal, we are making a decision to act. We are providing for ourselves a map and depending on the Lord to be our compass to point us in the direction He wants us to go! A goal is more than a dream, it's a dream acted upon. It's not saying "oh, I wish I could" it's declaring what we want to do for the Lord. It's a *declaration of faith!*

Let's seek God's will with Fasting & Prayer. He will make our lives interesting. Let's ask God as we set for ourselves a goal! Let's make a clear declaration of faith, saying "This is what I am going to do for the Lord and then press forward!" I can't wait to see where the Lord will take us!

Look and see where the Lord will take you when you have ***the will to press.***

**MEDITATION:** THOUGHTS, CONCEPTS, OR IMPRESSIONS FOR TODAY:

**RECORDING:** SIGNIFICANT EVENTS FROM TODAY'S DEVOTIONAL EXPERIENCE:

# Day 11

## *The Experience*

*Moses and Aaron, Nadab and Abihu, and the seventy elders of Israel went up and saw the God of Israel. Under his feet was something like a pavement made of lapis lazuli, as bright blue as the sky. But God did not raise his hand against these leaders of the Israelites; they saw God, and they ate and drank.*
*Exodus 24:9-11*

A God-given experience is just an experience if we do not allow it to translate into a life transforming experience. God gives us these experiences to transform our lives. When we allow this to happen these experiences will truly enrich our lives and become our personal transformation.

In Ex.24:9-11, the 70 elders of Israel, Aaron, Nabub, Abihu, Moses, and Joshua saw God and they ate and drank with Him. The Bible also states that God did not kill them (which is a good thing).

This was a fantastic experience for them. This experience should have been a life transformational experience for them. Sadly, it did not transform the lives of the 70 elders, Nabub, Abihu, and not even Aaron.

We know that when we read Ex.32:1-4, the people asked for a god of gold and a golden calf to be made for them to worship. None of these men stood up to oppose the people, to keep them from sinning. The experience on Mt. Sinai was given by God to transform these men into true leaders, not just men with titles.

But before we harshly judge these men, we must remember, it is as true for us today as it was for them. God gives us potentially transformational experiences and we, at times, do not allow those experiences to transform us.

We walk away, come from the mountain as it were, thinking that was a great experience and immediately start thinking, "What's for lunch?" or, "What's so and so doing after church?"

Some Christians become experience junkies. These are people who move from one God experience to the next, always looking for bigger and better experiences. They get that first rush or the high of the experience, but they soon crash, having no real satisfaction.

They do not allow these God experiences to transform them into the Lord's image. They do not allow themselves to be transformed, to be drawn closer to the Lord and to do the work of the ministry that they have been called to do. This is where we all find true satisfaction in the Lord.

We all need to allow these experiences to transform us. We do this by asking the Lord, "What is the specific purpose for us having the experience?" Then, we need to meditate on that purpose. Finally, we must ask the Lord to help us and allow the transformation to take place in our lives. The Lord Jesus has chosen each of us to be His people and He wants to transform us into a royal priesthood, a Holy Nation, that will transform the world in His name.

This is ***the Experience*** – to be transformed!

**MEDITATION:** THOUGHTS, CONCEPTS, OR IMPRESSIONS FOR TODAY:

**RECORDING:** SIGNIFICANT EVENTS FROM TODAY'S DEVOTIONAL EXPERIENCE:

# Day 12

## *Go Get It*

*"Brethren, I do not count myself to have [a]apprehended; but one thing I do, forgetting those things which are behind and reaching forward to those things which are ahead, I press toward the goal for the prize of the upward call of God in Christ Jesus."*
*Philippians 3:13-14*

What are athletes without goals? Goals are obstacles that help us reach higher levels of ability. In Philippians 3:14, Paul says we should keep running for the goal God has for us. In doing this, we all have to lean on the Lord to know where we are going.

As a believer, two elements are important when trying to reach our goals: focus and perseverance. Focus is "a state or condition permitting clear perception and understanding." Focus has to be steered in the right direction in order for you to reach your goal and, above all, God's will for your life. The second element, perseverance, is what I like to call "the ability to not quit, and to keep on going with a greater drive than you think you have." Perseverance is often a sown seed. As Paul states later, "If you don't give up you will reap a harvest in

God's timing." In action, perseverance gives life to character; character to hope and hope in Christ.

In life, we mess up, hit hurdles, overthink the goals, fall down, etc. I've seen many people get their minds stuck on one mistake and not let it go! We can't keep dwelling on the past failures; they will keep replaying in our minds until all we see is that one mistake, issue or fault.

So, today, when it feels like the devil is getting a foothold and trying to pull you down so that you can't glorify Christ, let's remember to fix our eyes on Jesus, our audience of One, who doesn't care if we mess up as long as we give our all to Him. Don't forget what God said, that He is doing a new thing, making all things new! Look forward to your goal. Forget past mistakes and look for a new opportunity to come. When it does, we'll be game ready for Christ's glory.

What is your goal today? ***Go get it!***

**MEDITATION:** THOUGHTS, CONCEPTS, OR IMPRESSIONS FOR TODAY:

**RECORDING:** SIGNIFICANT EVENTS FROM TODAY'S DEVOTIONAL EXPERIENCE:

# Day 13

## *Grace or Amazing Grace*

*And with great power the apostles gave*
*witness to the resurrection of the Lord Jesus.*
*And great grace was upon them all.*
*Acts 4:33*

When the disciples were left alone as Jesus ascended into heaven, a new beginning was just around the corner. Jesus told them to go to Jerusalem and wait for the Promise. That Promise came on the day of Pentecost, a day that would change their lives forever. God's Holy Spirit came upon them with sounds of a mighty wind that came from heaven, a demonstration of supernatural power. Tongues of fire were then dispersed on (sat on) each person (Acts 2:1-4). This event made it very clear that something amazing and indescribable was taking place amongst these people. In the days that followed this small group of believers came together in one accord, knowing that they had been given gifts from the Lord, and that they had been called to witness the gospel of the Lord Jesus Christ.

The first gift given involved "great power" as the apostles zealously told of their knowledge and personal experience of who Jesus Christ was and what He had done. The second gift, however, is one we sometimes take for granted but it is extremely crucial to the first one: "great grace." They were not only granted power but they were given great grace. Without grace, they could not go forth and do what they were called to do. The same is true for us today. We may have gifts, callings, knowledge, experience and all of the right answers, but without grace, we will not get very far in our service or our usefulness to God. Why? Because we will be taken out by our own thoughts and behaviors as human beings. We become too aware of our weaknesses and we try to overcome them in our own strength. We cannot control condemning thoughts of the enemy who tells us we are not worthy. We lose faith, hope and the eternal perspective because our focus shifts to ourselves. Grace, however, steps in and says that the Lord has granted us unmerited favor in His sight. He chose us. He loved us first. He called us to do His work. He gifted us for His purposes. Not of *us,* but of *Him,* by *His* grace.

Grace must accompany power in your life today. Grace must be connected to your faith. Do you understand the fullness of God's grace? Take time today and look up verses on "grace." Use your Bible concordance and just spend some time reading about grace. Make a study of it and take your time, even over several days. Let the Lord minister to you through His Word. If you are suffering or struggling, you need to approach His throne of grace with boldness and receive His mercy today. (Hebrews 4:16)

And even though we are not worthy, the Lord still uses us by giving us the gifts and grace to minister for Him and by Him and in Him. You will be blessed! Thank God for His ***amazing grace***

**MEDITATION:** THOUGHTS, CONCEPTS, OR IMPRESSIONS FOR TODAY:

**RECORDING:** SIGNIFICANT EVENTS FROM TODAY'S DEVOTIONAL EXPERIENCE:

# Day 14

## *Just a Touch Away*

*"One Touch is Enough"*
*Mark 5:21-42*

A woman in the crowd had suffered for twelve years with constant bleeding. She had suffered a great deal from many doctors, and over the years she had spent everything she had to pay them, but she had gotten no better. In fact, she had gotten worse. She had heard about Jesus, so she came up behind Him through the crowd and touched his robe. For she thought to herself, "If I can just touch his robe, I will be healed." Immediately the bleeding stopped, and she could feel in her body that she had been healed of her terrible condition. Mark 5:25-29 NLT

Jesus was walking down a crowded street to get to the home of a dying girl when a woman squeezed through the crowd and touched Him. As popular and well- loved as He was, I'm sure this had happened many times before but this touch was different. It was more than the touch of an adoring fan, it was a touch of faith. The woman had a hidden hurt that few knew about. She believed just touching Jesus could heal her. She was right.

Your need doesn't have to be the biggest one in the room for God to hear your prayer. The woman had an ailment that was bothersome, but apparently not life threatening. She'd had it for at least twelve years but it was minor compared to the need of a dying little girl. Our minor health issues, the tension in our marriage or our unhappiness at work seems insignificant compared to people we know who are dying from cancer, are all alone or out of work altogether. Our needs may seem small in comparison to the needs of others but that doesn't mean they are small to God. He cares just as much about us and our small needs as He cares about others and their big needs.

Often we're amazed at how many times God has calmed our hearts, eased our pains or given us a whole new perspective just through reaching out to touch Him. We may touch Him by reading His Word which then opens the door for Him to gives us clarity, revelation, and wisdom. We may touch Him by pouring out our heart to Him in faith-filled prayer which ushers in His presence, power and peace. It doesn't take hours of deep biblical study or days of repetitive supplication; sometimes all it takes is a touch.

Whatever your walking through today, big or small, He's near, He cares and He's just a touch away. Reach out with whatever faith you can muster and touch Him. Be amazed at what your Jesus can do with just a touch of faith. You are loved! Reach out- God is ***just a touch away.***

**MEDITATION:** THOUGHTS, CONCEPTS, OR IMPRESSIONS FOR TODAY:

**RECORDING:** SIGNIFICANT EVENTS FROM TODAY'S DEVOTIONAL EXPERIENCE:

# Day 15

## *Say Grace*

*Therefore being justified by faith, we have peace with God through our Lord Jesus Christ: By whom also we have access by faith into this grace wherein we stand, and rejoice in hope of the glory of God.*
*Romans 5:1-2*

Grace is far more than a mealtime prayer. The word communicates the idea of blessing. As children of God, we are the recipients of grace, which is poured out on us by our heavenly Father. Let's look at how we experience this benefit of His grace.

God's favor is seen in our salvation, as Ephesians 2:8 tells us: "For by grace you have been saved." The blessing is undeserved and unearned. He acted purely out of His goodness, sacrificing His precious Son Jesus Christ in our place. In that way, we could be reconciled to the Father and adopted into His family.

Grace is also the sphere in which we live the Christian life. At Calvary, we were transferred from the kingdom of darkness to the kingdom of light (Colossians 1:12- 13). Here, we live out our new identity as God's children and carry out His purpose of glorifying Him—both of which result in manifold blessings.

The beauty of grace becomes especially clear when we consider who we once were. We were spiritually dead, living according to our own selfish interests (Ephesians 2:1). But now, through faith in Jesus as our Savior, God has justified us and given us new life. He has declared that we have right standing before Him (Romans 8:1).

All of our sins were placed upon Jesus, and His righteousness has been credited to our account permanently.

Picture yourself living in the favor of God. Internalize this truth; then give Him thanks, ***say grace*** and receive it.

**MEDITATION:** THOUGHTS, CONCEPTS, OR IMPRESSIONS FOR TODAY:

**RECORDING:** SIGNIFICANT EVENTS FROM TODAY'S DEVOTIONAL EXPERIENCE:

# Day 16

## Make Room

*The Lord is near to all who call upon Him, to all who call upon Him in truth. He will fulfill the desire of those who fear Him; He also will hear their cry and save them.*
*Psalm 145:18-19*

Do you ever just feel so busy you don't even know what to do? If I'm not careful, my schedule can get out of control—and fast. I'm sure you know the feeling. It seems every other commercial on television or online depicts someone who has their life more put together than I do. All day long, we are bombarded with subtle messages telling us to do more and be more things to more people in more ways. It's exhausting.

As a culture, we are overloaded and distracted. How much time have you spent on social media today? How about your phone? How about in front of a computer? In today's world, distraction is par for the course—and it is robbing us of a deeper relationship with God.

I don't know what stage of life you find yourself in. Maybe you are working your way through school. Perhaps you are newly married or a recent parent trying to figure things out. Some of you may be deep in the trenches of marriage and raising children, and still others of you might have kids who are grown who now have kids of their own.

But regardless of where we find ourselves, know this: we are not alone in the challenges of our season, and we need God's presence in our lives to live our season well. We realize the distractions of today exceed our ability to have even imagined distractions in the past. Be encouraged to make intentional choices and make room for God. When we aren't hungry for God, it's time to stop for a moment and ask Him like the woman at the well, "Are you trying to fill your desires with other things, rather than allowing Jesus to fill you with His Living Water?"

Friend, Jesus is the source of all our life. Years from now, having a perfect house won't matter, that new Netflix series will be a thing of the distant past, the likes we get on social media will have lost their luster, and the time we've spent glued to a phone will be shown for the waste of time that it is.

You, my friend, are the gatekeeper of your world. We must choose carefully what we allow in. God wants to lead you into the secret place of His presence. You must remove distractions and ***make room*** for God.

**MEDITATION:** THOUGHTS, CONCEPTS, OR IMPRESSIONS FOR TODAY:

**RECORDING:** SIGNIFICANT EVENTS FROM TODAY'S DEVOTIONAL EXPERIENCE:

# Day 17

## *The Process of Life*

*Lord, who may dwell in your sanctuary? Who may live on your holy hill? He whose walk is blameless and who does what is righteous, who speaks the truth from his heart, and has no slander on his tongue, who does his neighbor no wrong, and casts no slur on his fellow man, who despises a vile man but honors those who fear the Lord…*
*Psalm 15*

The holy hill was the site of Jerusalem's temple. As the people made their way up to the temple, the place where they worshipped God, they were preparing to meet with God. David reflects on who may dwell in God's sanctuary and live in the Presence of God - one whose walk is blameless.

As the people ascended the mountain, perhaps it was a time when God was preparing their hearts to be with Him. God has made a way for Christians to approach Him today through His Son, Jesus Christ.

When we invite Him into our lives to dwell in us, He brings His kingdom and begins a process of transformation in us. Our spiritual journey is much like climbing a mountain, as reflected in today's Psalm. We accept Christ, and as we climb His mountain of transformation, we become more like Him.

In the Old Testament, only the High Priest could enter into the Most Holy Place. He did this once a year to offer sacrifices (atonement) for the sins of the people.

Jesus is our High Priest who has gone through the heavens to prepare an entrance into God's Presence: we do not have a high priest who is unable to sympathize with our weaknesses, but we have one who has been tempted in every way, just as we are - yet was without sin. Let us then approach the throne of grace with confidence, so that we may receive mercy and find grace to help us in our time of need. (Hebrews 4:15- 16)

Jesus, our High Priest, went before us on the holy hill where He died for our sins so that we might be able to approach God. Sinful man could not approach a holy God, and through His atonement on the cross, He made a way for us to approach a holy God. When He was lifted up on the cross at Calvary, He took our sin with Him and we can now approach the throne of grace with confidence.

The Lord is calling you to the mountain of holiness. His desire is for you to draw near to Him and to be holy as He is holy: Who may live on your holy hill? He whose walk is blameless and who does what is righteous. As we climb the mountain of holiness, and help us to lead a blameless, righteous life. Keep us from slander and from being deceitful ***in our process of life.***

**MEDITATION:** THOUGHTS, CONCEPTS, OR IMPRESSIONS FOR TODAY:

**RECORDING:** SIGNIFICANT EVENTS FROM TODAY'S DEVOTIONAL EXPERIENCE:

# Day 18

## *Positioned for Greater*

*Without a vision the people perish.*
*Proverbs 29:18*

God promises us an abundant life, but we can't have abundance unless we position ourselves in the greatness of God. We must have a vision of the greatness of God and pray to be God-focused rather than self-focused. If we are God-focused we can walk in true freedom. Then we can walk every day with a greater vision of what God is like, what He is saying, and what He can do.

The truth is that we are a desperate people. Before becoming a Christian, God would seem so far away and out of reach, but He will create a hunger in us to find truth. We knew there was a purpose to life and that we would find it someday. Many search for years and sometimes become quite desperate to find the answer to life. Eventually through reading the Bible, prayer or finding a spiritual mentor, you'll find the truth that sets you free. Jesus is our answer. The end of ourselves is the beginning of God. This is true of each one of us who know God personally. This is where we started and where we must live every day. We don't have it all together but God does. God wants to position us in the greatness of God. He wants to give us a new belief and expression of the power of prayer in our life. He wants to give us a new freedom in our walk with Him. God is preparing us. He wants to impart to us, 'new life'. His training is supernatural training. We are in the process of becoming. We are changed from glory to glory as we grow into a Christ- like person.

I have no second plan. But in the dark night as we desperately seek Him, we will find God. We come out of that desert leaning on God. In that quiet place we receive a greater vision of Who He is and a stronger belief in the power of prayer. God will bring you into a new dimension of victory.

Are you desperate today in some area of your life? Do you have questions where there are no answers but God? He uses ordinary people in extraordinary circumstances to show His mighty power. When you are desperate, you are in the prime place to shift into the greatness of God. Your impossibility opens the way for the possibilities of God – the very God who is greater than the universe and greater than every obstacle you may be facing. Desperation opens the way for the greatness of God. God has ***positioned you for greater!***

**MEDITATION:** THOUGHTS, CONCEPTS, OR IMPRESSIONS FOR TODAY:

**RECORDING:** SIGNIFICANT EVENTS FROM TODAY'S DEVOTIONAL EXPERIENCE:

# Day 19

## Call On the Lord

*Call upon Me in the day of trouble;*
*I will deliver you, and you shall glorify Me.*
*Psalm 50:15*

Sometimes there are people in our lives that we only see when they need something from us. But God is does not think that way towards us, His children. He desires for us to call Him when we need something. Our heavenly Father wants to hear from us in the middle of our problems and struggles as well as in our victories and triumphs. This verse contains three parts and all three are related to prayer.

The *first* is a command from God to, 'Call upon me in the day of trouble.' Certainly, we should not sit and wait until trouble comes to pray, but God's command is for us to pray in times of trouble. It may be that the trouble appeared to give God an opportunity to meet our need and for us to seek Him.

The *second* part is this amazing promise God makes that if we do call then, "I will deliver you." There are no limits how often we can pray. We still have the promise of His answer. It is a blessing to know that Gods hears and responds to our prayers. The *third* part is yet another promise from our Father, 'and you will glorify Me.' This may be the real reason for prayer in the grand overarching plan of heaven. Prayer is not only a mechanism we use for us to get rescued, but prayer is more about displaying God to the watching world. When God provides, even though we haven't prayed, we are tempted to forget God and think we have taken care of ourselves. But when we have prayed and He answers, then we recognize His hand of provision and are careful to honor (glorify) Him. We rob God of honor, and we do not glorify God when we forget it was Him who rescued us and provided for us. Today, don't forget to ***call on the Lord.***

**MEDITATION:** THOUGHTS, CONCEPTS, OR IMPRESSIONS FOR TODAY:

**RECORDING:** SIGNIFICANT EVENTS FROM TODAY'S DEVOTIONAL EXPERIENCE:

## Day 20

# So Far to Go

*Not that I have already attained, or am already perfected; but I press on, that I may lay hold of that for which Christ Jesus has also laid hold of me.*
*Philippians 3:12*

There is a sign along an airport runway that says, "Keep moving. If you stop, you are in danger and a danger to those who are flying."

The same could be said of Christians. We always need to keep moving forward spiritually. We cannot rest on our laurels.

Even the apostle Paul said he could not live off his past experiences. He needed to keep moving forward. He said, "Not that I have already attained, or am already perfected; but I press on, that I may lay hold of that for which Christ Jesus has also laid hold of me" (Philippians 3:12). Here was one of the greatest Christians of all time saying that he had not yet attained. He was saying, "I have not arrived at some supernatural plane that is not available to other believers. I have so far to go."

If anybody ever knew God, it was the apostle Paul. He had led countless people to faith. He had established churches. He had written epistles. Yet he said of himself that he had so much to learn and so far to go.

Although Paul among many could boast of his devotion and inspiration of God, he wrote many letters to the churches, wrote most of the New Testament and suffered for the faith even unto death.

Yet he did not boast. He said, "I have not attained. I have so far to go." Just as The Apostle Paul shared how far we still have to go. We too, like him, can say, "We have ***so far to go."***

**MEDITATION:** THOUGHTS, CONCEPTS, OR IMPRESSIONS FOR TODAY:

**RECORDING:** SIGNIFICANT EVENTS FROM TODAY'S DEVOTIONAL EXPERIENCE:

# Day 21

## *One Thing*

*One thing I have desired of the Lord, that will I seek: that I may dwell in the house of the Lord all the days of my life, to behold the beauty of the Lord, and to inquire in His temple.*
*Palam 27:4*

Every day we can focus on One Thing; staying devoted to Christ with all our heart. God will show us challenges we need to overcome or something about how we live our daily lives that needs to change so that we can get more centered on Christ as our One Thing.

The Bible records how some of our unlikely heroes inspire us to live with singular devotion to the Lord. One good example is that of Mary: She set aside her kitchen work to sit at Jesus' feet and listen to Him and she received his affirmation.

Now, let's seek the One Thing that is the best thing, - to be more devoted to Christ. Don't you want more of Him? A greater closeness with Him? Of course you do or you wouldn't be reading this Devotion!

So, how do we grow to be devoted to Christ as our One Thing? How do we make real changes to how we live our daily lives as an expression of love for God? How do we overcome worry or anger? How do we learn to rejoice in trials? Do we pray without ceasing? Can we love difficult people? We can try hard, but that won't last very long. The way to make a real character change - to learn, grow, or heal in any area - is by training. Look to Jesus as your Coach and "work out" with Him. "Train yourself to be godly" as Paul advises us (1 Timothy 4:7). An important part of any spiritual training program is *meditating* on Scripture.

To *meditate* on Scripture is more than reading it. And it's different than studying it. When you meditate on Scripture you pray through God's Word by applying it to the struggles and opportunities of your life. You become as a bee that stops on a flower and lingers, staying on the flower to suck out the nectar and using it to make sweet honey. "Your word, O Lord, is sweeter than honey!" exclaims the Psalmist (Psalm 119:103, my paraphrase).

May you and I, day-by-day, discover more sweetness in Scripture and use it to live for the ***One Thing*** of loving God and loving others as He loves us.

**MEDITATION:** THOUGHTS, CONCEPTS, OR IMPRESSIONS FOR TODAY:

**RECORDING:** SIGNIFICANT EVENTS FROM TODAY'S DEVOTIONAL EXPERIENCE:

## Day 22

# The Ultimate Prize

*Being confident of this very thing, that*
*He who has begun a good work in you will*
*complete it until the day of Jesus Christ*
*Philippians 1:6*

Our life is like a long distance run or race and we're all participating in it. Jesus will equip us for this Journey called Life. Sometimes on this journey you might have to pivot, bend, turn and adjust in unique ways - that you never had before. The Ultimate Prize is Jesus is on this journey with you, perfecting that which concerns you.

We've run into peaks and valleys along the way, but we keep running. There are times the route takes an uncertain turn, the terrain gets a little rocky and there may have been times along the way when you fall and hit the dirt, but you get up and keep running. The race of our life is much longer than the longest marathon. And it's an uneven path. There are many opportunities to become tripped up as we live in this world day to day.

The Apostle Paul of Philippians offers us a sweet remembrance that the best way to run this race of life is by keeping our eyes on Jesus. Jesus is the person on whom our faith depends from the very start of our race until the end. Our race on earth will end only when we die or when Jesus comes to take us away in the rapture, whichever comes first. It is only by keeping focused on Him that we have any chance of living the kind of life that God calls each of us to live. Jesus tells us that He came into the world so that all people could have an abundant and full life (**John 10:10**). Paul describes what a full life looks like when he lists the Fruit of the Spirit in **Galatians 5:22-23**. These "fruits" become evident when the Spirit of Jesus is manifested in our lives.

As we regularly reflect on what Jesus did on the cross so that our sins can be forgiven - which makes it possible for us to have a relationship with God - we are encouraged and don't get weary in our race. We need to stay close and abide in Jesus so that we can draw strength from Him so that His Spirit is reflected in our lives. (John 15:5) I have identified this as an essential **Spiritual Exercise** for a healthier life.

Each step you take, every conversation you have, each glance you take - all your actions and behaviors - is a part of your race here on earth. We can only run and finish our race well if we keep our eyes on Jesus, ***the ultimate prize.***

**MEDITATION:** THOUGHTS, CONCEPTS, OR IMPRESSIONS FOR TODAY:

**RECORDING:** SIGNIFICANT EVENTS FROM TODAY'S DEVOTIONAL EXPERIENCE:

## Day 23

# *Prayer Is Key*

*Call to Me, and I will answer you, and show you great and mighty things, which you do not know.*
*Jeremiah 33:3*

Prayer and faith is the formula, and standing on the word of God moves mountains in our lives. Often times, we look for other possibilities to find a way of escape, and release answers to various situations that arise in our lives. The key to all our situations rest in the ultimate communication with the only true and living Savior. The key to the ultimate communication is prayer.

Have you ever found a key laying around your house or office area, and you ponder "What does this key go to?" Well, with God in prayer, you will never have to wonder what key reaches heaven. You will never have to wonder what key moves heaven; you will never have to wonder what key words to say to God. **Prayer** is the key to reach heaven. Faith moves heaven and the Word of God is what we echo to reach heaven.

Psalms 103 reminds us, to never forget all His benefits. Hebrews 11:6 reminds us, without faith it's impossible to please God. Luke 18:1 reminds us, that we ought to always pray and not faint.

Prayer can take you to heights unknown; it can change the atmosphere. Shadrach, Meshach and Abednego can attest to how the keys of prayer, praise and faith (determination) unlocked the fiery furnace, (Daniel 3:10 -28). The woman with the issue of blood was healed with the key of faith. Her determination to touch the hem of Jesus' garment made her whole. Jehoshaphat and his army won the battle with prayer and fasting, (II Chronicles 20).

Paul reminds us that the weapons of our warfare are not carnal but mighty in God through the pulling down of strongholds, (II Corinthians 10:4). How do we pull down the strong holds of the enemy? By having the full armor of God, (Ephesians 6:18-20). Having these primary elements, you can maintain a relationship with Jesus Christ.

Hold on to your key! Never worry about losing them. They're embedded in us. All it takes is to commune with Jesus Christ, have faith and stand on the Holy Word of God. Remember today, ***prayer is key***.

**MEDITATION:** THOUGHTS, CONCEPTS, OR IMPRESSIONS FOR TODAY:

**RECORDING:** SIGNIFICANT EVENTS FROM TODAY'S DEVOTIONAL EXPERIENCE:

# Day 24

## *Guard Your Mind*

*Do not be deceived, my beloved brethren.*
*James 1:16*

In many, if not most cases, temptation enters through the doorway of our minds. When Satan wanted to lead the first man and woman into sin, he started by attacking the woman's mind. That is why Paul warned the Corinthian believers, "But I fear, lest somehow, as the serpent deceived Eve by his craftiness, so your minds may be corrupted from the simplicity that is in Christ" (2 Corinthians 11:3).

We need to protect our minds. This is where the enemy will hit us, because we can reach into the past through our memories and into the future through our imaginations.

When the children of Israel were in the wilderness, their first step into trouble was looking back. God had miraculously delivered them from Egypt. He fed them with manna from Heaven every day. Granted, it was manna <u>every single day</u>. They had tried all of the recipes in Moses' cookbook, *101 Ways to Eat Manna*. But they remembered the food they had in Egypt. Isn't it interesting that they thought it was a lot better than it really had been? They let their imaginations run wild as they remembered the scraps of food that were given to them by the Egyptians and then magnified those scraps into feasts.

That is how the devil will try to work against us. He will make a few good times we had seem like the greatest times we ever had. But he is a liar. Jesus said, "No one, having put his hand to the plow, and looking back, is fit for the kingdom of God" (Luke 9:62). So don't look back.

Temptation starts with a thought, and the tempter needs cooperation from the tempted. That is why we need to ***guard our minds.***

**MEDITATION:** THOUGHTS, CONCEPTS, OR IMPRESSIONS FOR TODAY:

**RECORDING:** SIGNIFICANT EVENTS FROM TODAY'S DEVOTIONAL EXPERIENCE:

# Day 25

## *Focused Attacks*

*And these are the ones by the wayside where the word is sown. When they hear, Satan comes immediately and takes away the word that was sown in their hearts.*
*Mark 4:15*

Temptation comes to everyone, but the enemy focuses many of his attacks on those who are young in the faith and those who are making a difference in the kingdom.

After our conversion the devil is there, tempting us to doubt our own salvation. He whispers in our ears, "You think you are saved? You think Christ really came into your life? Are you crazy?" This is just a tactic the enemy keeps recycling again and again.

The Bible tells us that when we are young in the faith, we are especially vulnerable. We see in the parable of the sower that young believers are immediately attacked. Jesus said, "And these are the ones by the wayside where the word is sown. When they hear, Satan comes immediately and takes away the word that was sown in their hearts" (Mark 4:15). He is there to attack those who are young in the faith.

Temptation also comes to those who are making a difference in the kingdom of God. First of all, he doesn't want you to come to Christ. But once you have made that commitment, his next strategy is to immobilize you, to get you to compromise yourself and be ineffective. He doesn't want you to be a threat to his kingdom.

If you want to make a difference, if you want to reach people who don't know the Lord, then don't expect a standing ovation in Hell. The enemy won't take it lightly. He will attack you. You had better expect it. Brace yourself for it, and have a ***focused attack***. Pray for other believers, whether they are new in the faith or are already making a difference.

**MEDITATION:** THOUGHTS, CONCEPTS, OR IMPRESSIONS FOR TODAY:

**RECORDING:** SIGNIFICANT EVENTS FROM TODAY'S DEVOTIONAL EXPERIENCE:

# Day 26

## *An Opportune Time*

*Now when the devil had ended every temptation, he departed from Him until an opportune time.*
*Luke 4:13*

In a broad sense, temptation can come to us at any time. Of course, it often happens after times of great blessing. Jesus was tested, or tempted, in the wilderness for 40 days and nights, right after His baptism in the Jordan River when the Spirit of God came upon Him in the form of a dove. After the dove came the devil. After the blessing came the attack. Often after great times of blessing, the enemy will be there, wanting to rob us of what God has done.

Maybe you have experienced a great time of blessing in your life recently. Enjoy it, but keep your guard up. The enemy will be there. He will attack you. And he will tempt you. He waits for the opportune time to attack, and we are often the most vulnerable when we think we are the strongest.

If you think that weak believers had better be careful, then I have a thought for you: Strong believers had better be careful too. The Bible says, "Therefore let him who thinks he stands take heed lest he fall" (1 Corinthians 10:12).

Many times temptation can come when we are relaxing. Take David for example. He was tempted when he was up on the rooftop taking a little rest and relaxation, at the time when kings usually go out to battle. He noticed the beautiful Bathsheba as she was bathing on her rooftop, he lowered his guard, and he made one bad decision that led to another. He had Bathsheba brought to him, had her husband killed and took her as his own wife.

There is no rest from the spiritual battle. Always stay prayed up, because the moment you think, *It won't hit me here,* that is when something can hit you. The enemy is waiting for ***an opportune time***. This is an opportune time for you - keep on your armor. Prayer is a mighty shield for the enemy's attacks.

**MEDITATION:** THOUGHTS, CONCEPTS, OR IMPRESSIONS FOR TODAY:

**RECORDING:** SIGNIFICANT EVENTS FROM TODAY'S DEVOTIONAL EXPERIENCE:

## Day 27

# *Just Our Nature*

*But each one is tempted when he is drawn
away by his own desires and enticed.
James 1:4*

We all know what it is like to be tempted. But where does temptation come from? It does not come from God. James 1:13-14 says, "Let no one say when he is tempted, 'I am tempted by God'; for God cannot be tempted by evil, nor does He Himself tempt anyone. But each one is tempted when he is drawn away by his own desires and enticed." We play a key role in our own temptation.

We must be careful and at the moment of temptation, consider that God always gives us a way of escape. It is not the Lord that tempts us, but that within that draws our desires elsewhere. One could say this does not bother me, yet another is hindered by the same thing. Our desires are to be given over to the Lord in prayer.

We can come to God and ask Him to help us and like a good father, He does. Our human nature was born into sin and can be a hindrance to the work of God. But because our God being The Righteous One, causes us to seek Him and bring to Him even our desires that they may be clean and pure. Oh, how great is our God? He is greater than any temptation, stumbling block or hindrance put before us. Are there areas of temptation that you need God's help in overcoming? Seek Him? He will help you.

**MEDITATION:** THOUGHTS, CONCEPTS, OR IMPRESSIONS FOR TODAY:

**RECORDING:** SIGNIFICANT EVENTS FROM TODAY'S DEVOTIONAL EXPERIENCE:

# Day 28

## *Too Busy to Serve?*

*Then another of His disciples said to Him, "Lord, let me first go and bury my father." But Jesus said to him, "Follow Me, and let the dead bury their own dead."*
*Matthew 8:21-22*

If the devil can't hinder our relationship with God by making us immoral, he'll simply make us too busy. All we have to do is look around today to see the evidence of this sad truth. Our busy lifestyle is making us less healthy, too. We push ourselves past the point at which our bodies and minds function properly, and we often suffer for it with headaches, stomachaches, anxiety and depression. This is not God's way. The Bible says, "A calm and undisturbed mind and heart are the life and health of the body." (Proverbs 14:30 AMP) Walking in the peace that Christ died for us to have will enable us to walk in the wholeness that is His perfect will for us. Besides costing us our health and peace of mind, busyness can cost us our God-ordained relationships. When we are feeling rushed, pressured and preoccupied, we are destined to mistreat the people around us. As a result, our relationships with our spouses, children, parents, and friends will suffer. Most importantly, our relationship with God will suffer.

The Bible indicates that we will eventually answer to God for what kept us busy while we lived on this earth. We must ask ourselves, "What am I giving my attention to? What keeps me busy?" We need to ask the Lord, "What do You want me to change? What would You have me leave alone?" Jesus told His disciples, "We must work the works of Him Who sent Me and be busy with His business while it is daylight." (John 9:4 AMP) Notice that the Savior said that WE must be busy with God's business. Every child of God has an earthly assignment and purpose, and it's up to us to discover it and perform it as we walk in close fellowship with Him on a daily basis.

If you are living an *overly-busy* lifestyle today, the Lord is calling you to make some changes, and He doesn't expect you to make them alone. He says: "Come to Me. Get away with Me and you'll recover your life. I'll show you how to take a real rest. “Walk with Me and work with Me”, says God - watch how I do it. Learn the unforced rhythms of grace." (Matthew 11:28,29 MSG) Today, spend time in the Savior's presence and in His Word, and let Him teach you how to follow in His footsteps of purpose, passion and peace! You are not ***too busy to serve***.

**MEDITATION:** THOUGHTS, CONCEPTS, OR IMPRESSIONS FOR TODAY:

**RECORDING:** SIGNIFICANT EVENTS FROM TODAY'S DEVOTIONAL EXPERIENCE:

## Day 29

# Counting the Cost

*And whoever does not bear his cross and come after Me cannot be My disciple. For which of you, intending to build a tower, does not sit down first and count the cost, whether he has enough to finish it. . . .*
*Luke 14:28*

When Jesus was in Jerusalem during the Passover, John's Gospel tells us that many believed in His name after they saw the miracles He performed. But Jesus did not entrust himself to them, because "He knew all men, and had no need that anyone should testify of man, for He knew what was in man" (John 2:24-25).

There are lots of people who say they want to follow Jesus and that is good. But that commitment will be challenged. We must decide to follow Jesus not because our best friend, boyfriend or girlfriend follows Jesus. Not because our parents follow Jesus, but because **we** have chosen to follow Christ.

Many of us can get caught up in the moment. But do we realize the hours, days, months, and our very lives that God is seeking after in dedication to Him? We aren't to love God today and serve Him, then turn away and do our own thing. His love is a lifetime commitment to us.

We get excited about the good things. But are we willing to go through the hard things? Are we willing to count the cost? Is our commitment to Him and Him alone? Are we willing to be real followers of Jesus?

The same can happen to us. God might speak to our hearts about serving Him more. And we respond, "Lord, I love You. I check in every Sunday. I put a little something in the offering. But I don't have time to go out and do those extra things. I am so busy."

If you haven't discovered the joy of serving God, then you are missing out. There is something for everyone to do in service to Him. Don't miss out on that.

God loves us and desires to bless us. What treasures have you discovered through your relationship with God? This will help you ***count the cost*** of serving God.

**MEDITATION:** THOUGHTS, CONCEPTS, OR IMPRESSIONS FOR TODAY:

**RECORDING:** SIGNIFICANT EVENTS FROM TODAY'S DEVOTIONAL EXPERIENCE:

## Day 30

# For Our Good

*For this is the love of God,*
*that we keep His commandments.*
*And His commandments are not burdensome.*
*1 John 5:3*

When we look around we see that the world has perfected the art of **performance-based** love. It is exhausting to feel like you're only as valuable as you are expendable. The good news is that our performance does not determine Jesus' love for us.

It can be difficult to wrap our minds around how Jesus loves. We easily fall into the habit of performance, view Jesus' commands as *rules* to follow instead of a means to *intimacy* with Him. But 1 John 5:3 says it is out of love for Jesus that we obey His rules – not the other way around. God's commands have not been put into place to *oppress* us, but to *free* us. God's plan for our lives is the best plan for our lives. So when we give God ultimate control, it gives us **ultimate joy.**

If we measure our value on how well we're following the rules, we make our faith about **us** instead of Jesus' death on the cross. Obedience is not about how we *perform,* but how we *respond*. We say yes to God because we love Him, not out of obligation to Him or because we want something from Him.

Obedience is as simple as listening to Jesus and doing what He says. Don't follow the rules – follow Jesus.

Have you ever thought that God valued your performance over your position as His child? Did that mindset make you feel free or burdened? Think about the most joyful times in your walk with Jesus. Were they a result of obedience? Consider these things as you pray today. What God asks of us is ***for our good***.

**MEDITATION:** THOUGHTS, CONCEPTS, OR IMPRESSIONS FOR TODAY:

**RECORDING:** SIGNIFICANT EVENTS FROM TODAY'S DEVOTIONAL EXPERIENCE:

# Day 31

## *Jesus Christ, Our Anchor*

*"This hope we have as an anchor of the soul, both sure and steadfast, and which enters the Presence behind the veil."*
*Hebrews 6:19*

We have an anchor in Jesus Christ through the power of prayer. That anchor is steadfast and unmovable.

The anchor we can depend on that will never leave us or forsake us. The power of prayer is the power that comes to us when we realized that God can be our anchor in the midst of our circumstances. Our God is greater than any situation that we may encounter in our daily lives.

It's the power that comes when we're able to be centered, anchored in a belief and rooted in a Truth which is stronger and deeper than the day-to-day truths we struggle with. In the book of Ephesians Apostle Paul wrote to the people of Ephesus, about God's desire for us "that we may no longer be children, tossed to and fro and carried about with every wind of doctrine, by the cunning of people, by their craftiness in deceitful wiles." (Ephesians 4:14) In prayer our hearts and minds can be focused on the eternal truths of God and not the changing, indecisive truths of human reasoning and human nature.

Hebrews 6:19 reminds us "this hope we have as an anchor of the soul, both sure and steadfast, and which enters the presence beyond the veil" Our hope in Christ is firm and secure. The anchor of God is strong enough to support his people under their heaviest trials. Let us, therefore, set our affections on things above, and wait patiently for His power to manifest in our lives.

Hold on with faith, to ***Jesus Christ, our anchor,*** and the ultimate communication we have in the **Power of Prayer**!

**MEDITATION:** THOUGHTS, CONCEPTS, OR IMPRESSIONS FOR TODAY:

**RECORDING:** SIGNIFICANT EVENTS FROM TODAY'S DEVOTIONAL EXPERIENCE:

# *Prayer List*

*With thanksgiving, let your requests*
*be made known to God.*
*Philippians 4:6*

| Prayer Request | Prayer Answered ☑ |
|---|---|
| | |
| | |
| | |
| | |
| | |
| | |
| | |
| | |
| | |
| | |
| | |
| | |
| | |
| | |

# *For Added Meditation*

## THE ATTRIBUTES, NATURE, And NAMES OF GOD

1. **Holiness:** God's moral excellence and perfection.
2. **Righteousness:** The complete moral excellence and perfect justice of all that God does.
3. **Immutability:** The unchangeableness of God; He is forever the same.
4. **Eternity:** God transcends time and possesses the whole of His life all at once.
5. **Omnipotence:** God is almighty and possesses total and complete power.
6. **Omniscience:** God is all-knowing.
7. **Omnipresence:** God is everywhere present at the same time.
8. **Wisdom:** God always chooses and wills the best means to attain the ends He has in view.
9. **Goodness:** God is bountiful and kind to all His creatures.
10. **Love:** The unconditional attitude and affection that God manifests toward His creatures.

11. **Grace:** The unmerited favor of God to those who have forfeited it.
12. **Mercy:** The loving withholding of punishment and retribution from those in Christ.
13. **Longsuffering:** The patience of God with His creatures.
14. **Faithfulness:** The total trustworthiness of God.
15. **Independence:** The self-existence of God. He exists because He is God and does not depend on anything outside of Himself.
16. **Infinity:** God is totally above measure.
17. **Truth:** God is the source of all truth.
18. **Revelation:** God has lovingly revealed Himself to man through His creation, man's conscience, His Word and His Son.
19. **Sovereignty:** God rules totally in all the affairs of His creation.
20. **Solidarity:** There is only one God.
21. **Trinity:** The one God has revealed Himself to us in three persons: the Father, the Son, and the Holy Spirit.
22. **Spirituality:** God is immaterial and invisible.
23. **Majesty:** The unique excellence of the manifest glory and supremacy of God.

24. **Elohim:** God's official title. He is God!
25. **Jehovah:** God's covenant name with Israel, pronounced Yaweh in Hebrew. It is formed from the Hebrew verb meaning "I AM."
26. **Adonai:** Lord and Owner of all.
27. **El Shaddai:** The Almighty God; literally, "The God who is more than enough."
28. **Jehovah-Jireh:** The Lord, the Provider (Genesis 22:14).
29. **Jehovah-Rapha:** The Lord, the Healer (Exodus 15:26).
30. **Jehovah-Nissi:** The Lord, the Banner of Victory (Exodus 17:15).
31. **Jehovah-M'Kaddesh:** The Lord, the Sanctifier (Leviticus 20:7, 8).
32. **Jehovah-Shalom:** The Lord, my Peace (Judges 6:24).
33. **Jehovah-Tsidkenu:** The Lord, my Righteousness (Jeremiah 23:6).
34. **Jehovah-Shammah:** The Lord who is there (Ezekiel 48:35).
35. **Jehovah-Rohi:** The Lord, my Shepherd (Psalms 23:1).
36. **Jehovah-Sabaoth:** The Lord of Hosts (I Samuel 1:3).
37. **Lord:** God is the Master of everything.
38. **King:** God's sovereign rule in His kingdom and His total creation

39. **Messiah/Christ:** The Anointed One.

40. **Savior:** The One who brings salvation.

41. **Immanuel:** God with us.

42. **The Word:** Jesus as the Divine Communication of God to man.

43. **Mediator:** Jesus as our High Priest, interceding with the Father.

44. **Lamb of God:** Jesus as the approved sacrifice for our sins.

45. **The Rock:** God is our stability and protection.

46. **Alpha:** The first letter of the Greek alphabet. It signifies God as the beginning of all things.

47. **Omega:** The last letter of the Greek alphabet. It signifies God as the end of all things.

48. **The Living One:** The God who is alive and the Source of all life.

49. **Abba Father:** God is my "Papa God" through Christ. He is an intimate God.

50. **The Light of the World:** Jesus as the illuminator of God and His Truth.

51. **Bread of Life:** Jesus as the Satisfier of man's soul

# *About the Author*

## Tracy Jackson

Tracy Jackson's devotional writings are personal sermon notes, reflections from her daily quiet time of Bible reading, prayers, and journal entries. She is blessed to have a supportive husband, Larry Jackson. As well, Tracy enjoys her role of motherhood and is blessed to have four children: Tyler, Joshua, Ezekiel and Ashley.

Tracy resides in Kansas City, Missouri and is a member of Trinity Temple Church of God in Christ- where she serves as the Prayer Director. As a servant of Jesus Christ, Tracy is devoted to serving her church and community. In addition to faithfully serving in her local church, she also has a personal "Power of Prayer" Ministry. She sponsors a complimentary Prayer Breakfast Experience once a year—via personal invitation in which attendees come at no cost. The gathering is non-denominational; her mission is centered on uniting believers to stand in the gap for one another in prayer, thanksgiving and exhortation to the wounded.

Her Kingdom purpose is Christ focused/centered, and her life's mission is to be a servant of Jesus Christ.

# *Power of Prayer Ministry*

## *Our Mission*

*As believers in Christ we should never feel that we are alone. Believers at all levels of spirituality, come together in an informal time of fellowship and prayer with thanksgiving.*

## *Ministry Statement*

*The Power of Prayer Ministry is to unite believers to stand in the gap for one another in prayer, knowing that God is a rewarder of those who diligently seek Him.*

***"... Men ought always to pray and not faint." Luke 18:1***

*Rejoice evermore. Pray without ceasing. In everything give thanks: for this is the will of God in Christ Jesus concerning you. 1 Thessalonians 5:16-18*

**CONNECT WITH THE MINISTRY**

**Online:** www.PowerofPrayerExperience.com

**Email:** tracyj27@att.net

Sow into this ministry via cash app: $tracy4prayer